ANIMAL LIVES

MARGARET LANE is a naturalist and author of the biography of Beatrix Potter. In this new series, she combines her knowledge of wildlife with her understanding of children. What does a new-born fox cub look like? Where do foxes make their secret lairs? The answers to many questions are presented in a realistic story that will intrigue young imaginations. Detailed and superbly naturalistic illustrations make this book a perfect introduction to the life of the fox.

Additional titles:

THE FROG   THE SQUIRREL   THE FISH
THE BEAVER   THE SPIDER

To Sam Parkes   M.L.

To Sarah-Jane, Joanna and Matthew   K.L.

First published in Great Britain 1982
by Methuen Children's Books Ltd
in association with Walker Books
First published in Picture Lions 1985
by William Collins Sons & Co Ltd
8 Grafton Street, London W1

Printed in Great Britain
by William Collins Sons & Co Ltd, Glasgow

THE FOX

By Margaret Lane

Illustrations by
Kenneth Lilly

FONTANA
PICTURE LIONS

The fox lives by his wits. If he were not immensely clever he would have disappeared long ago, like the wolf and the wild cat. As it is, due to his own skill and cunning the Red or Common Fox is doing very well indeed in Britain and Europe, in North America and North Africa. Man is his only enemy, and the fox has worked out a great many sensible methods of living comfortably close to him without being found out.

The fox is a nocturnal animal.
That is to say, he comes out of hiding
after dark, having spent the day sleeping
in an 'earth' – a hole in a sandy bank or
among the roots of a tree – or some other
hiding-place under brambles and bracken.
Like a cat, he can see pretty well in the
dark and his hearing is wonderfully sharp,
a great deal better than ours. And his
sense of smell is so keen that his moist
black nose, quivering to the least breath
of wind, tells him all he needs to know.

Foxes do not live permanently in families. The male, or dog fox, is on the whole a solitary animal, ranging about in an area that he knows well and regards as his own. It is the female fox, the vixen, who feeds and looks after her cubs until they are old enough to hunt and survive by themselves. She, unlike the dog fox, may keep to a particular earth for quite long periods, perhaps even two or three years. She is not fond of hard digging, so usually takes over a hole dug by rabbits or badgers, and enlarges it to suit her own ideas.

The dog fox and the vixen look
exactly alike. Their coat is thick and
reddish or yellowish-brown, with
creamy-white hindquarters and
underparts and a fine tail or 'brush'
which often has a white tip. The ears,
legs and feet are almost black. The cubs,
when small, have shorter muzzles,
dark brown woolly coats and little
pointed tails, rather like kittens.
But at three months old they begin to
look like their parents, and before
long wander off to find hunting grounds
for themselves.

The foxes' breeding time is in winter, when the vixen makes her weird calls, which sound like the scream of a peacock. This is a signal to all dog foxes in the neighbourhood, who quickly make their way to her patch and fiercely fight one another, rearing on their hind legs and gnashing their teeth. She may mate with more than one, but the courting season is brief. The vixen ceases to call and the dog foxes depart. The dominant male may stay in the area for a while, without sharing the earth or taking much interest in his mate.

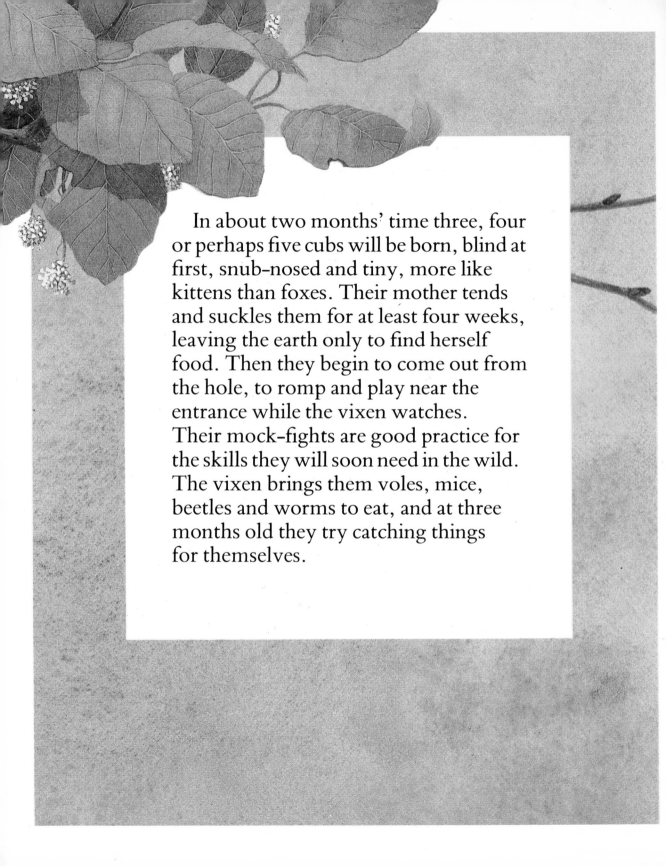

In about two months' time three, four or perhaps five cubs will be born, blind at first, snub-nosed and tiny, more like kittens than foxes. Their mother tends and suckles them for at least four weeks, leaving the earth only to find herself food. Then they begin to come out from the hole, to romp and play near the entrance while the vixen watches. Their mock-fights are good practice for the skills they will soon need in the wild. The vixen brings them voles, mice, beetles and worms to eat, and at three months old they try catching things for themselves.

Foxes lead fairly solitary lives because food is hard to come by and each one needs his separate hunting ground. Rabbits are a favourite meal, but they are hard to catch. Rats, voles, mice and frogs are easier prey, and birds that nest on the ground. Foxes eat eggs when they can find them and dig beetles out of cowpats. They also like ripe blackberries in autumn, and in farming country a straying duck or hen is a great prize. This makes the farmer the fox's enemy, and the game-keeper too, since man kills and eats pheasants and is furious when fox or vixen does the same.

Luckily for the fox, his sense of smell is so keen that he can catch the scent of a man a long way off. He knows who, or what, is in his area simply by his nose. Both sexes leave their own scent everywhere as well, partly by urinating on bushes and posts, partly through scent–glands in the pads of their feet. These scents enable hounds to follow the fox through fields and hedges, often for great distances. Without them, they would never find his private paths and lairs, which he knows like a map, and which are well hidden.

Fox-hunting is not as old a sport as many people believe. In earlier times it was the hare and the deer that provided sport for man, horse and hound. In those days there were not enough foxes to be worth chasing, but as time went on they increased and fox-hunting became popular. It is not an easy sport, for the fox has his own methods of escape. He may cunningly mingle with a flock of sheep, run along a motorway or swim across ponds and streams to conceal his powerful scent.

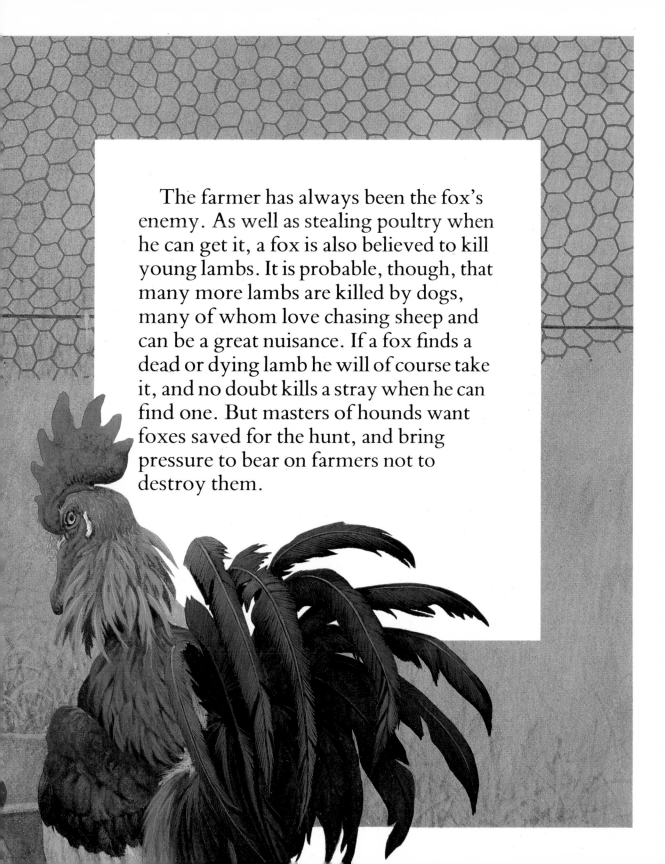

The farmer has always been the fox's enemy. As well as stealing poultry when he can get it, a fox is also believed to kill young lambs. It is probable, though, that many more lambs are killed by dogs, many of whom love chasing sheep and can be a great nuisance. If a fox finds a dead or dying lamb he will of course take it, and no doubt kills a stray when he can find one. But masters of hounds want foxes saved for the hunt, and bring pressure to bear on farmers not to destroy them.

So foxes, through the years, have become more numerous, although thousands are still hunted and killed each year. The fox uses his wits, as usual, and as human populations increase and towns grow bigger he has discovered that he can live quite well in the suburbs, where there are neither hunts nor game-keepers, and food can be snatched from dustbins and rubbish-heaps, as well as from rabbit-hutches, bird-tables and fish-ponds in back gardens.

Many people living near towns and motor-roads would be astonished to learn that the fox may be a near neighbour. He is so clever at keeping out of sight, so quiet, so cautious that they would never believe he goes through their dustbins in the dark, haunts cafés and lay–bys, catches rats by their chicken-run or potting–shed and spends the day in a secret lair not a stone's throw away, curled up like a cat with his thick soft brush tucked snugly over his nose.

FONTANA
PICTURE LIONS